IMAGES OF ENGLAND

AROUND
HACKENTHORPE

IMAGES OF ENGLAND

AROUND
HACKENTHORPE

LEONARD WIDDOWSON

TEMPUS

Frontispiece: Hackenthorpe newsagent's shop on the village green.
From left to right: Percy Rippon (owner), Herbert Staniforth, Fred
Unwin, Hedley Hibbert, Reg Rippon.

First published 2003

Tempus Publishing Limited
The Mill, Brimscombe Port,
Stroud, Gloucestershire, GL5 2QG
www.tempus-publishing.com

British Library Cataloguing in Publication Data.
A catalogue record for this book is available from the British Library.

ISBN 0 7524 3061 0

Typesetting and origination by Tempus Publishing Limited
Printed in Great Britain by Midway Colour Print, Wiltshire

Contents

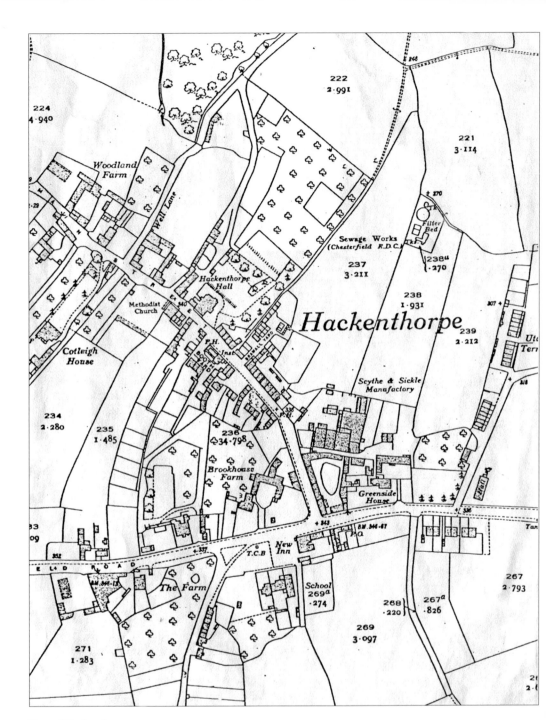

Plan of Hackenthorpe.

Introduction

A Roll of Entreats of Grants from the year 1291 mentions a Norf Gilbert Hacun and his wife, Margaret, living in Thorpe within the Beighton Manor. As 'thorpe' is an old Norse word meaning a hamlet or farmstead, this family named Hacun may well be the origin of the name of Hackenthorpe.

In common with most places, the agricultural system of open fields was worked in Hackenthorpe in ancient times. This involved the cultivation of large fields with a complete absence of hedges, where each man of the village had his strip or furlong of land for ploughing, usually with an ox. In Hackenthorpe, there were three such fields. Firstly, there was the East Field, where the Hogshead public house now stands. Church Lane was the old track that gave access from the road. The second was Mill Field, which stretched from Carr Forge Dam up to the end of Main Street, where the social club and old library building is. The third field was called Scourdings and this was where today's Scowerdons estate is. The access track followed the old Spa Lane, which was the continuation of Main Street and is now Dyke Vale Road.

Hackenthorpe occupied a frontier position as it is situated on the border of the ancient kingdoms of Mercia and Northumbria. The Shirebrook at the bottom of the Scowerdons estate was part of this boundary. It also formed part of the boundary between the ecclesiastical sees of York and Canterbury, and until 1966 was part of the border between Yorkshire and Derbyshire. In more local terms, it separated the parishes of Handsworth Woodhouse and Beighton. At the eastern end, the Battle of Brunnanburgh was fought in the Rother Valley in 937, and it was to the west at nearby Dore where King Egbert is said to have been crowned as the very first King of all England in 829.

At the height of the nineteenth-century industrialisation, there were five edge-tool grinding sites – these were the Shirebrook, the Upper Sickle Wheel, the Lower Sickle Wheel, the Carr Forge Scythe Wheel, the Rainbow Forge and the Cliff Dyke Wheels used by Thomas Staniforth's. Charcoal was produced locally to supply the forges. Birley

West coal pit was sunk in 1855 and Birley East in 1888. In 1855, a two-and-three-quarter-mile railway line was laid from Woodhouse Junction to Birley West, which was used by both pits.

In 1725, Lord Harley travelled from Sheffield to Welbeck, and his route took him over the Shirebrook at Birley Vale and over Birley Moor. He wrote: "I came upon the greatest number of wild stunted holly trees that I ever saw together." This was due to the trees being constantly lopped to browse sheep. Nearby Hollinsend gets its name from those long-gone trees. The word Birley is derived from 'burh' – an old English word meaning a fortified area – and 'leah' – meaning a clearing. It is interesting to note the significance of a fort here, close to the Shirebrook.

The Romans were certainly present in these parts. From their fort at Templeborough they made a road, called Ricknield Street, to the next fort south at Chesterfield. Part of this road passed over Birley Moor, quite close to Birley Spa. When the Hackenthorpe estate was being built in 1952, the late Mr Leslie Butcher (an archaeologist) made a significant find of over twenty Stone Age flints close to Birley Spa. These dated from the Mesolithic Period (3,000 to 8,000 years ago), proving that early Stone Age man was here all that time ago.

Not bad when it was said that little has happened and there cannot be any early history here.

L. Widdowson
October 2003

Acknowledgements

To all those who have helped me to produce this book, I am very grateful, especially to Brian Newbolt for the pre-print typesetting from my handwritten captions for the pictures. Thanks also to others, including Brian, who have loaned me the photographs – Ben Clayton; Peter Wolstenholme; Cathy Murphy; Margaret Willows and friends; the Siddall family of Aptos, California, for two pictures from the booklet *The Continuing Story of St Cyprians*; the late H.V. Garside, for an illustration and two photographs; Gillian Bramhall, for her 1938 copy of the Thomas Staniforth catalogue; and the Beighton Local History Society.

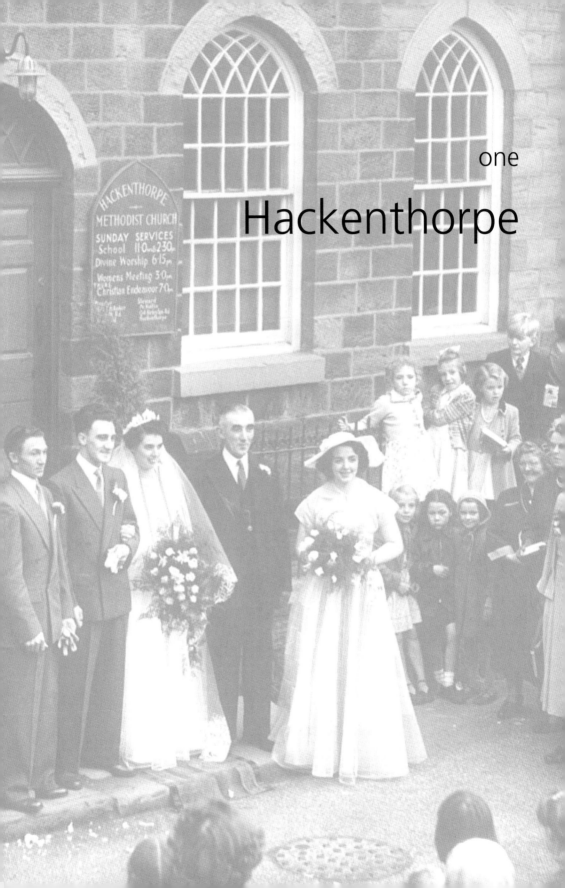

one

Hackenthorpe

HACKENTHORPE
METHODIST CHURCH
SUNDAY SERVICES
School 11.0 and 2.30pm
Divine Worship 6.15pm
Womens Meeting 3.0pm
Christian Endeavour 7.0pm

An aerial view of Brookhouse Farm, when Horace Spencer lived there, *c.* 1960.

Eric Keeton in the doorway of the No. 8 Branch, Handsworth Woodhouse Co-operative shop in 1926. Before 1899, this was the mission church.

Above: The two-storey
extension gave more
floor area for the present
occupants, of Charles
Singleton Ltd.

Right: The wall
plaque.

The name Church Lane has been retained.

Greenside was built by Thomas Staniforth, *c.* 1825.

From the gateway of Greenside, along Sheffield Road, can be seen the post office, the old blacksmith's forge and the veterinary surgery.

New houses being built on the site of the old village school.

Fairmount nursery and pre-school, 1994. This was once the late Dr De Domball's residence and surgery, which he built when he left his home in Robin Lane, Beighton. On retirement, he went to live on the South Coast.

Thomas Staniforth's building has now been converted into shops, a dentist's and some small workshop units.

In 1960 Staniforths were taken over by Edge Tool Industries of Birmingham. In 1967 a new company was formed. Spearwell Tools Ltd., comprising Edward Ewell, Brades, Skelton & Tyzack and the garden tool section of Spear & Jackson. The sickle production went to a subsidiary company, George Booth & Sons. Eventually the works closed, and all production stopped in 1980.

Some of Thomas Staniforth's employees, around 1910. From left to right, back row: William Sargent, Ernest Needham, Harry Havenhand, Walter Autram, Ernest Parkin, Albert Clark. Middle row: Walter Sargent, Alfred Crookes, William Boland, Charlie Pickering, William Hardwicke, Horatio Needham, William Unwin, ? Graddon, Charlie Helliwell (manager). Front row: Charlie Wragg, Arthur Needham, Albert Fowler, Willis Pashley, William Hutchinson, John Thomas Needham, ? Crookes, ? Heind, Windsor Needham.

Above: The managers and their families at an agricultural show.

Left: The cover of the 1938 Thomas Staniforth catalogue.

Opposite: The company letterhead and managing director's remarks.

Also Sole Proprietors of
the Names and Marks :
"CASTLE & TURTON"

C. T
(Regd.)

JOHN RILEY & SONS
(Regd.)

W. FOX & SONS
Corporate Mark
L O
(Regd.)

THOS. STANIFORTH & Co Ltd.
"SEVERQUICK"
TRADE MARK

MANUFACTURERS OF

GARDEN & EDGE
TOOLS — SCYTHES
HATCHETS & HOOKS
BUTCHERS' CLEAVERS

SINCE 1743.

SEVERQUICK WORKS, HACKENTHORPE
SHEFFIELD.

STANIFORTH'S
SEVERQUICK
REGISTERED TRADE MARK.

October 14th, 1937.

NEW PRICES.

Dear Sir,

We invite you to study carefully the pages of our G.L. 38 Price List.

At present we can allow you a SPECIAL 15% discount as shown on the attached sheet (subject to certain reservations.)

How long this will last we cannot say, owing to steel prices.

We would stongly advise you to place your business with us for next season without delay.

Thanking you,

Yours faithfully,

Thos. Staniforth & Co. Ltd.

Managing Director.

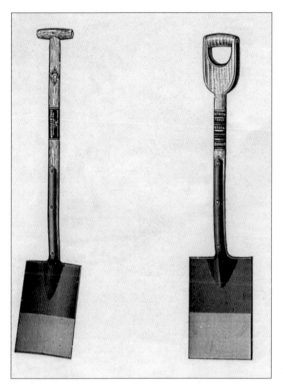

Two spades.

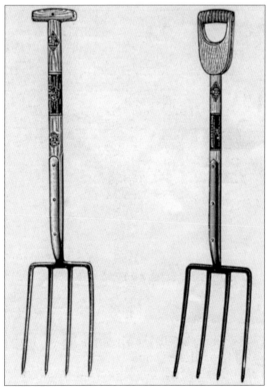

Two forks.

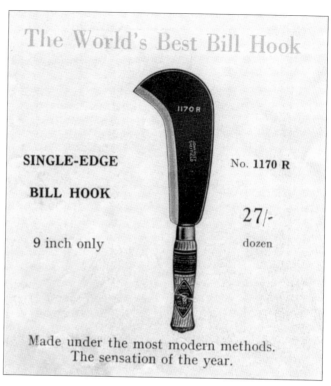

The World's Best Bill Hook

SINGLE-EDGE

BILL HOOK

No. 1170 R

27/-

9 inch only   dozen

Made under the most modern methods.
The sensation of the year.

The world's best billhooks.

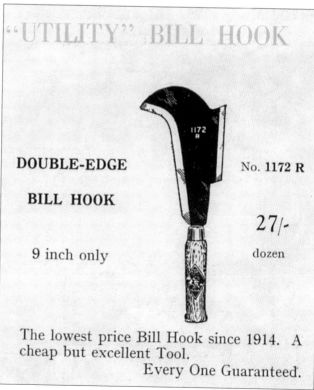

"UTILITY" BILL HOOK

DOUBLE-EDGE

BILL HOOK

No. 1172 R

27/-

9 inch only   dozen

The lowest price Bill Hook since 1914. A
cheap but excellent Tool.

Every One Guaranteed.

A utility billhook.

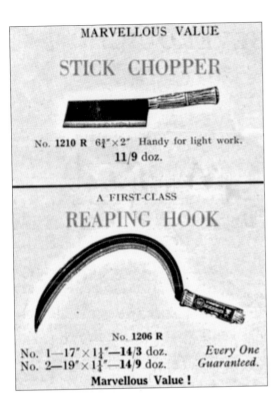

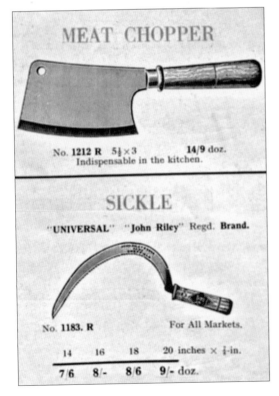

A stick chopper and a reaping hook.

A meat chopper and a sickle.

'LITTLE WONDER' HATCHET

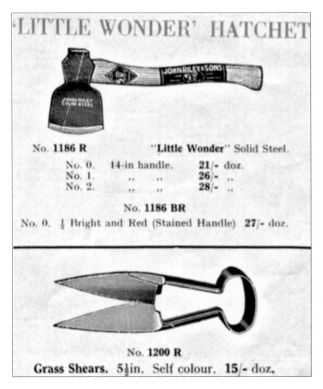

No. 1186 R   "Little Wonder" Solid Steel.

No. 0.   14-in handle.   **21/-** doz.
No. 1.   ,,   ,,   **26/-** ,,
No. 2.   ,,   ,,   **28/-** ,,

No. 1186 BR

No. 0. ¼ Bright and Red (Stained Handle) **27/-** doz.

Grass Shears. 5½in. Self colour. **15/-** doz.
No. 1200 R

Left: A hatchet and some grass shears.

Below left: A Norwegian scythette and some pruners.

Below right: Some ner-break scythes.

NORWEGIAN SCYTHETTE

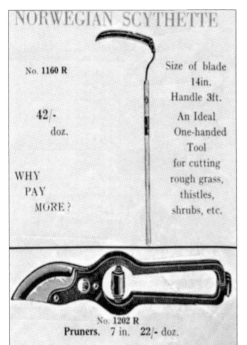

No. 1160 R

42/- doz.

WHY PAY MORE?

Size of blade 14in.
Handle 3ft.
An Ideal One-handed Tool for cutting rough grass, thistles, shrubs, etc.

Pruners. 7 in. **22/-** doz.
No. 1202 R

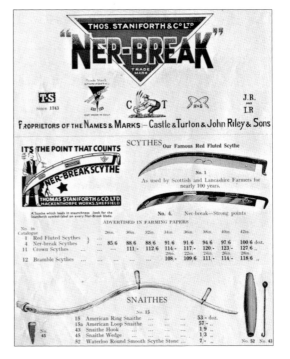

Around twenty-five men, women and children, pictured in the year 1895.

The same or a very similar group outside the village shop.

Main Street, with the old Blue Bell public house on the left. The row of houses was built by Thomas Staniforth's for the families of their employees.

At the far end of Main Street, c. 1900. Every building and tree has long since gone. A pharmacy and a doctors' surgery are on the near left-hand side now. Cotleigh Road now joins Main Street where the house on the left is.

Only the cottage, Hackenthorpe Hall and the tall building beyond the row of five houses have survived to the present day.

Ena Rippon and Brian Newbolt were the first couple to be married at the now-demolished Methodist church in its 125-year history. The church stood opposite the cottage of Hackenthorpe Hall.

Marjorie Webb is crowned May Queen, 1937. Doris Hague, the retiring May Queen, is on her right. The happy, smiling faces of the retinue include Hilda Hunt, Brenda Naylor, Mary Middleton, Ena Rippon, Elsie Fox, Kath Hunt, Ivy Pettitt, Rita Lambert and Idris Gingle. The gentleman in the cap is Mr Little and the other man is the caretaker of Hackenthorpe Hall. The little boy carrying the crown is Tom Platts.

Hackenthorpe Hall was rebuilt by James Hounsfield.

The panel over the doorway displays the initials of James Hounsfield and the year 1875.

Hackenthorpe Hall today. After being rebuilt and extended, the alterations have been so extensive that very little of the old hall can now be seen.

This board shows the present usage.

James Hounsfield also built and fitted up a workmen's leisure room in 1892-93, which was known as the reading room. It contained a games room, a full-size billiards table and a reading room 'to have a regular supply of daily papers'. The village men elected a committee to run the club, and a nominal rent of one shilling a year was paid to James Hounsfield, who was also the president. The two pictures show its present use as a carpet shop, and before that as a cycle shop, rented by Howard Wyers.

Left: Opposite the hall is this pair of three-storey houses. They are the only other properties by the roadside of the old village.

Hackenthorpe Library, closed in 1995, was re-located within Waterthorpe Library, Crystal Peaks.

The Hackenthorpe Garden Society's hut has also gone.

The Hackenthorpe Social Club.

Construction of the Mosborough Parkway in 1986. The bridge takes the path from Rainbow Forge to the Hackenthorpe housing estate.

This Hackenthorpe branch of the Sheffield Co-operative Society closed its doors on 16 June 1994.

Along with the development of the Hackenthorpe housing estate, it was necessary to demolish the old Sportsman public house. This much larger new building, set twenty yards behind the old one, replaced it during the mid-1950s.

A mixed and wide-ranging age group of people outside the old Blue Bell, *c.* 1900.

The present Blue Bell replaced the old one when it was rebuilt and greatly extended in 1955.

Part of the old building can be seen from the car park.

Hackenthorpe cricket team. From left to right, back row: umpire J. Carnell, Jack Bramall, Sam Staniforth, Cyril Binney, Sidney Holmes, Arnie Frith, Joe Lilley, Albert Taylor, Eric Havenhand. Front row: Bernard Hunt, Harry Helliwell, Jim Outram, Stan Hunt, Harry Barker, Lewis Frith.

Managers and staff of Thomas Staniforth's Severquick Works. This photograph was taken on 12 May 1937, and a copy was presented to every member of staff by Geo. Thos. Carter, the managing director, as a souvenir of the Coronation.

The old farmyard of Brookhouse Farm and dovecote building. Most of these are now private dwellings.

Inkersall House and workshops, pictured when the Five-Star Engineering firm was there. Inkersall House is a Grade Two listed building, but detached houses now occupy the rest of the site.

Above: The New Inn, known locally as Betsey's, after Betsey Helliwell. In 1959, the licence was withdrawn and the property sold for private purposes. On 20 July 1959, the licence was transferred to the Golden Plover on Spa View Road. The building was bought by J.F. Whittlestone, a veterinary surgeon, who changed the name to New Court.

Opposite above: The business is now owned by A. Crookes & Partners.

Opposite below: The village infants school, which existed from 1880 until 1991. The first two headteachers were Margaret Handley and Alice Burns. Then, in 1883, Mr H.B. Lund took over as headteacher when the school was enlarged. He served there for forty years, retiring in December 1922. He was followed by W.E. Turner (1923), S.V. Hanford (1930), Miss A.M. Knowles (1943), M.E. Payne (1954), S. Sutton (1954-55), Mrs A. Butler (1955) and Mrs Y. Hardwick (1966). Finally, Mrs S. Oliver was headteacher from 1988 until the school's closure in 1991.

Hackenthorpe Infant School board.

The playground behind the school, just before demolition.

No longer does the school bell ring
to call the pupils to school.

Mr Harry B. Lund, headmaster of the
school, with his staff of four
schoolteachers. Unfortunately, the
names of the ladies are not given, but
the one seated on the right can be seen
with Mr Lund in a group photograph
from 1922. She is dressed in exactly the
same way (including wearing the long
string of beads pictured here) and can be
identified as a Miss Fox.

Hackenthorpe pupils with two adults in 1922. From left to right, back row: Elizabeth Allen, Nora Sharpe, Bessy Barker, Winnie Hill, Ruth Carnall, Ethel Hunt, Bill Lancaster, Eric Milson. Second row: Florence Royston, Geoffrey Lilley, Charlie Sykes, Leslie Harris, Roland Hill, Billy Woodman, George Wyers, Roy Ayers. Third row: Tommy Edwards, Stanley Hunt, -?-, ? Roberts, Miss Fox, Harry B. Lund (headteacher), Louie Pearson, Nellie Havenhand. Fourth row: Walter Barker, Eddie Webb, Joseph Lilley, Herbert Massey, Cyril Binney, Jim Taylor, Willis Staniforth, Ernest Sanderson. Front row (seated): Freddie Taylor, Dick Jenkinson, George Wade, ? Wells, John Bartholomew.

Hackenthorpe pupils with teacher Mrs Stewart, 1929/30. From left to right, among the pupils on the back row are: Iris Dickinson, Betty Platts, Phoebe Chapman, Alice Carnall, Dorothy Sargeant. Second row: Joyce Outram, Arthur Thompson, Reg Gingell, Tom Crookes, Tom Liversidge, Roland Madin, Bill Smith, Sadie Thompson, Mrs Stewart (teacher). Third row: Barbara Taylor, Edith Pilley, Mary Brown, Joan Staton, -?-, Ivy Hinsley, Connie Bentley (Walters), Marion Holmes. Among the pupils on the front row: Douglas Sargent, Ron Chapman, Cecil Thompson, Eric Redfern, Midge Etches, Charlie Barnes, Ken Thompson.

An 1884 group photograph with Mr Lund on the left. The two lady schoolteachers must surely have dressed for the occasion.

Hackenthorpe Cricket Club with the Norton and District Trophy, which they won in 1938. From left to right, among the players on the back row are: J. Bramall, Jim Taylor, Ken Thompson, Stan Fenton, umpire. Front row: Lew Frith, Ray Shaw, Arnie Frith, Jim Outram, Albert Taylor, S. Staniforth, Ken Paddison, umpire.

The fox hunt assembles on the village green.

Percy Rippon (in Army uniform) and George Platts, pictured around the time of the First World War.

Mr Robert Helliwell standing with a horse and rider, just before they leave for the hunt.

Above: Sheffield Road in 1948. On the left is Helliwell's Farm, opposite that is Hounsfield's Farm and, in the distance, the New Inn.

Left: This red-brick house, No.4 Sheffield Road, was built for the coachman of William James Le Tall, who was a surgeon from Woodhouse and came to live at Inkersall House in January 1880. He gathered and published a few historical notes on Woodhouse and District and played a prominent part in local affairs.

A 1960s photograph of Hackenthorpe church. The dedication took place on 11 November 1899, when the Lord Bishop of the Diocese of Southwell, the Right Reverend George Riddings, officiated. On 3 June 1898, the foundation stone was laid by Viscount Newark. Beneath this stone is a casket, containing a coin of the realm, a newspaper of the day and a parchment bearing the names of the church committee. The cost of the building was £2,550.

Hackenthorpe church from above the road, before the alterations.

The church with its new doorway.

A 1930s group of schoolboys, pictured with the headmaster, after winning a trophy for the best-kept school garden. From left to right, back row: -?-, Ken Barnes, Leslie Littlewood, Mr Sidney V. Handford (headteacher), B. Lilley, Roland Madin. Front row: Bob Mathews, -?-, Walter H. Smith, Reg Gingells, Tom Liversidge. Seated: Doug Sargent. Walter Smith's name can be seen on the war memorial *(opposite page)*. He lost his life on 24 May 1941, along with 1,400 others, when HMS *Hood* was sunk by the German battleship *Bismark*.

The war memorial in the grounds of Christ Church, Hackenthorpe.

1939·WORLD·WAR·1945· ·1914·THE·GREAT·WAR·1919·

WALTER H. SMITH.	1941,	REGINALD TAGG. 1916,
DOUGLAS N.B. BARKER.	1942.	CLIFFORD RENSHAW, 1916,
GEORGE LILLEY,	1943.	BENJAMIN CROOKES. 1917,
RICHARD BRISTOW.	1943.	HARRY B. OXLEY. 1917,
WILLIAM H. SHAW.	1944.	EDWARD GRADDEN. 1918,
ARTHUR THOMPSON.	1944.	FRED ELLIS. 1918,
GLADSTONE POYNTOR.	1944.	JOHN ROSE, 1919,

"THEY DIED THAT WE MIGHT LIVE."

The new church hall built on the south side of Christ Church.

Cotleigh cottages. A pair of stone-built cottages on the opposite side of the road to the church. 'Cotleigh' was an ancient field name, which was also adopted by the now-demolished Cotleigh House. This was a Hounsfield family Georgian-style residence, situated off Cotleigh Road near the end of Main Street.

These gateposts are just to the left of Cotleigh cottages. They were placed there in 1939 for a driveway to be made to Cotleigh House, but due to the outbreak of war, and the demolition of Cotleigh House when Sheffield Council bought the land for housing after the war ended, the driveway was never done.

Donetsk Way is named in recognition of Sheffield's twin city in the Ukraine and was opened on 6 September 1982 by Councillor A. Michael Peat.

Before the Hackenthorpe supertram stop was constructed, work was proceeding at the end of Donetsk Way in October 1993. Cotleigh cottages and the church are on the left of the picture.

A supertram at the Hackenthorpe stop in September 1995, looking west to Sheffield Road and the Birley golf course.

A part of Sheffield Road after the tramlines had been laid in September 1993.

The same place as the previous photograph, *c.* 1900. The junction of Occupation Lane can be seen on the left opposite Throstlenest Farm, and Christ Church stands prominently in the background.

The Rainbow Forge Primary School infants' buildings in 1996. Detached houses now occupy this site.

Birley Spa Junior School in November 1998. This has also been demolished, but it has been replaced by a much larger building to the left on what used to be a part of the playing field.

The Rainbow mini-market and off-licence, and the small bus shelter at the old Hackenthorpe bus terminus of the No. 41 route. The shop closed shortly after this photograph was taken in 1993, probably due to the close proximity of the Crystal Peaks shopping centre. The Hogshead public house is on the right.

This Mainline bus was brought out of retirement in 1996 to provide a temporary free bus service to Sheffield in December of that year.

The Golden Plover public house, on the corner of Birley Spa Lane and Spa View Road, which opened on 20 July 1959 after the licence was transferred from the New Inn in the village.

Our Lady of Lourdes Church on Springwater Avenue. The Jesuit priests (from Spinkhill) had served Beighton, but then on Sunday 22 February 1953, a new Catholic parish was created and based at this newly-built church in Hackenthorpe. Father Peter McDonagh became the new parish priest. He served until 1971, when he was succeeded by Father Oliver Wilson.

two

Moorhole and Owlthorpe

Above: Moorhole Farm was demolished after John Pratt and his family moved to Spinkhill Hall Farm in around 1984.

Right: All the old buildings in this section of the book can be found on the 1899 Ordnance Survey map.

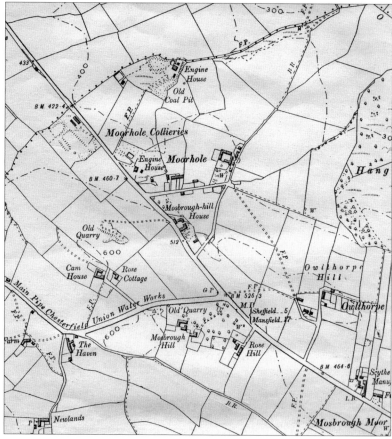

This row of six cottages at Moor Valley– Nos 20 to 25 – was built in the late nineteenth century when the Moorhole Collieries were across the road. It was known locally as Diamond Row, due to the chimney stacks being built at a forty-five degree angle to the row of houses. Note the oval iron plates providing support for the end wall.

This picture shows how the chimney stacks are offset and have not been built in the more traditional way of square-on to the row of houses.

The Birley Moor garden centre at Diamond Row, Moor Valley, Moorhole, which was built on the site of the old Dent Main Colliery.

The buildings in 1997, just before demolition. These were used as engine houses for the Moorhole Collieries.

Looking in a westerly direction along the A616, with the cleared site where the engine houses used to be on the right.

Detached houses now occupy the grounds and are collectively named Moor Valley Close.

The bored holes in the large stones at the entrance to Moor Valley Close are a reminder of when their use was to firmly secure the machinery in the colliery buildings.

These cottages on the left hand side of the lane were demolished after the Second World War.

This cottage on the right of Moorhole Lane, known as Christmas Cottage, stands alone, having survived the fate of its neighbours which have all been pulled down.

The house's oval plaque – it's a pity the bird is not a robin.

Another view of Moorhole Farm, *c.* 1970.

Mosborough Hill House. This was the residence of Richard Swallow JP, nineteenth-century colliery owner, and later John F. Swallow. It can be seen from the map that it was built on a triangular piece of ground, 512 feet above sea level.

Two imposing cannon guard the eastern approaches to the house.

This unusual-shaped stile can be found at the junction of the three dotted-lined footpaths on Owlthorpe Hill.

Wilson's garage at Moorhole, January 1988.

The right hand house was a public house, the Fitzwilliam Arms. It closed in the 1930s, the licence being transferred to the Birley Hotel (see page 88).

Above: This new detached house now occupies the site where the pair of semi-detatched houses on page 64 once stood. On the wall of the building on the left is a rare, wall-mounted Victorian letter box.

Right: Here, the Victorian letter box is pictured still in its original position and having been recently painted. It is marked on the 1899 map by LB.

The British Oak public house on Mosborough Moor was built around 1825 by John Cowley, sickle manufacturer, as a private house.

Owlthorpe Hill, as seen in 1994 from Bridle Stile. Houses are now built on the rest of the land to the right and, despite strong public opposition, this farmland (as well as Rose Hill) on the left has also been used for housing (see map).

Moor Farm, as seen from Owlthorpe.

The Mosborough side of Moor Farm. The map shows it to have been used as a scythe and sickle manufactory.

This field shows the black circles of soil where charcoal burning took place, *c.* 1990. Taken from Donetsk Way, part of Hanging Lea Wood is visible at the top right corner of the photograph. 'Hanging' means 'sloping' in this context.

Looking back down from the top of the field. These black patches can best be seen when it has been recently ploughed.

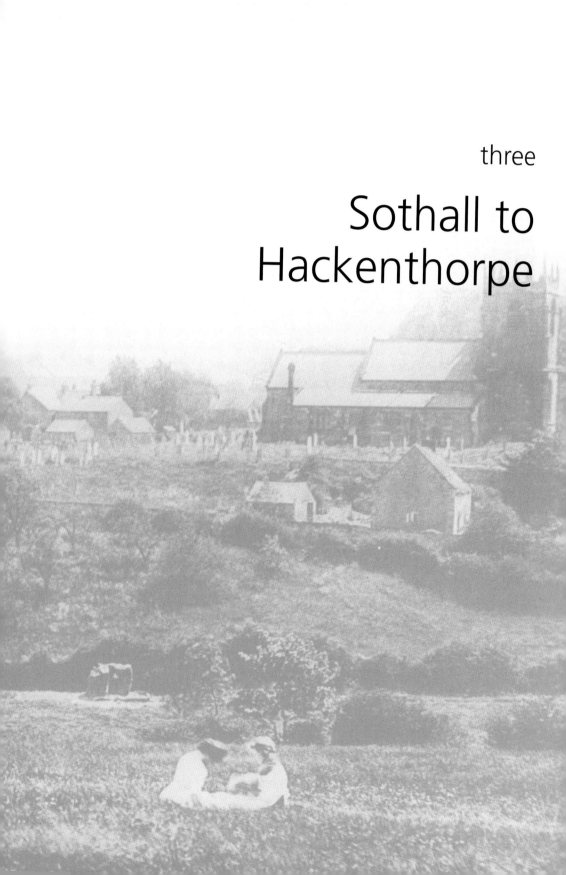

three

Sothall to
Hackenthorpe

Drakehouse Lane at Sothall, *c.* 1900. The numerous cart tracks show up in the lane's earth surface. The new Gypsy Queen public house and car park now cover the field on the left hand side.

The public house and restaurant from the south car park, which opened in December 1998.

Above: The opposite side, seen from Drakehouse Lane.

Left: The pub's sign board. Would Lucretia, Queen of the Gypsies, have approved of the picture?

The cottage below Beighton Church, sadly long since gone, was where Lucretia lived. Her gravestone has the following inscription: "To the memory of Lucretia Smith, Queen of the Gypsies, who died 20 November 1844, aged seventy-two years." It can be found close to the path which comes down from the church.

Sevenairs Road. This name was chosen because a local doctor used to say to some of his patients: "Walk to the top of these fields and breathe in the pure air. There are seven airs and it will do you more good than any medicine I can prescribe."

Young children with their balloons have come from school to see the lord mayor open the market. The soon-to-be-demolished Drakehouse can be seen through the trees.

The lord mayor of Sheffield, Mrs Dorothy Walton.

Some of these trees are still here, opposite where Drakehouse stood. The ploughed field has since disappeared in the building of Crystal Peaks.

Opposite above: Mrs Walton performs the traditional cutting of the red ribbon to declare the market officially open. The gentleman to her right is ready to clap his hands and begin the applause.

Opposite below: This was the third Drakehouse to occupy this site and gave Drakehouse Lane its name. Following an eighteen-month period in 1986-87, when the land was used as an open-air market, it is now an overspill car park for the Crystal Peaks shopping complex.

The bus station at Crystal Peaks.

Part of Crystal Peaks and one of its five car parks. The bus station is off the picture to the right.

Also gone is Chiwali Farm, which has been replaced by crossroads and traffic lights. Turn right for the car parks and bus station, and left for the Drakehouse retail park.

This bungalow had to go. It was one of the two belonging to the Ling family, and both buildings stood in the way of the retail park development.

An advertisment from the post-war period when G.H. Ling had extensive nurseries here.

Located just beyond Ling's and known as the school houses, this used to be a school for children from Hackenthorpe and Beighton between 1855 and 1880. Earl Manvers, who was the Lord of the Manor, gave this one-acre site for a school and a headmaster's house. At first, this school was run on a monitor system, where the master – a Mr Daniel – instructed a number of the brighter pupils to teach the rest of the children. Later on, adult teachers were employed. John Bickel, who was headmaster in 1879, was transferred to the new school at Beighton in 1880. The school was then converted into houses, and, after more than eighty years, these were demolished in the 1960s.

Above and below: Both of these bungalows, Moss View and Drylands, were doomed. They were demolished along with both Ling family homes in 1992. The Stanley Tools factory now occupies the land.

Looking down the road towards Moss View and Drylands in 1991. The old school houses stood where the large trees are now, and the Lings' bungalows were opposite the electricity pylon.

The Stanley Tools factory. Notice the concrete gateposts of Moss View, which are still there today in the hedgerow.

Above and below: Part of the Drakehouse retail park.

Carter Lodge School and playing fields. This has now been renamed Rainbow Forge School after the previous school had to close.

The Milestone public house, complete with a milestone featuring the inscription: "The Milestone, opened 15 December 1988. Banks Brewery, Wolverhampton, seventy-nine miles."

The Hackenthorpe station of the South Yorkshire Police on Moss Way, built in 1995.

Peaks Centre, the Sheffield College, opened in 1999.

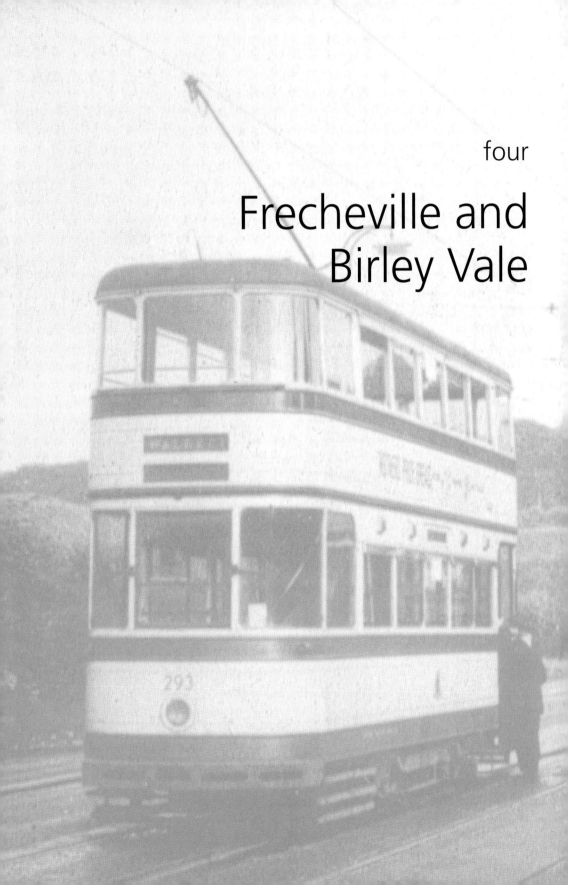

four

Frecheville and
Birley Vale

The No.9 branch of the Woodhouse Co-op, built for the Frecheville estate in the 1930s, was taken over by the Brightside & Carbrook Co-operative Society, along with all the other branch shops, in around 1967. This picture was taken when it was owned by the Sheffield Co-operative Society, just before its demolition in June 1988.

Barclays Bank was also lost within a few days of the Co-op's demise.

Within eighteen weeks, the new store was built, stocked and ready to open.

Mr Twigg, the president of the Sheffield Co-operative Society, cuts the red ribbon on
28 October 1988 as the queue of people, after listening to his address, stand patiently waiting to
go into this modern store.

The Birley Hotel, also built in the 1930s, was a Mappins house – Mappins were brewers of Masbrough in Rotherham. As explained on page sixty-four, it acquired its licence from the Fitzwilliam Arms at Mosborough. Older residents will remember the clock which used to be on the top right hand corner of the photograph and displayed 'Mappins Beers' instead of numerals. Stones Brewery took over Mappins in 1954.

Opposite the Birley and the Co-op was the Spa club. Its doors were closed for the last time shortly after this photograph was taken in September 1990.

Now extended, with a new frontage added and renamed the Sherwood, the former Spa club is seen here in July 1991.

Opposite the top of Heathfield Road, in Churchdale Road, is the Frecheville community centre. Sir Enoch Hill JP, FCIS, opened the community centre at 3 p.m. on Monday 21 June 1937. Among the many celebrities to come here before the war was the snooker king, Joe Davies, who played a match against Charlie Simpson.

Also on Churchdale Road is St Cyprian's church, consecrated by the Bishop of Derby on 31 May 1952.

The side doorway of the church.

Left: The panel above the side door and the spire of St James' church, at Derwent, the ruins of which lie under the water of Ladybower reservoir.

Below: Some of the old pews from Derwent, which came to St Cyprian's.

Above: The altar at St Cyprian's, May 1991.

Left: The organ, built by Brindley & Foster of Sheffield in 1903. In 1968, T.C. Wilcock made extensive repairs as well as some additions to the instrument.

Above: Part of the interior of Derwent Church. Note the lectern (now at St Cyprian's) and the pews on the right, which appear on page ninety-one.

Right: Another view of the church shows the chancel, the nave and the decor.

Beryl Young and Joan Hay are busy cleaning the church brasses.

Gwen Rawson crowns the carnival queen Pat Eyre (now Hartley) in 1953, outside the community centre. The queen is pictured with her page boy and young lady attendant. Mr Bigford stands behind the chair.

Inside the community centre is Pat Eyre (centre) with Mr Bigford, Mr Guylee and, on the right, Eaton Davies.

Class Two, Frecheville Junior School, 1941. From left to right, back row: Mr Chambers (headteacher), Joan Brown, Pat Cummner, Maureen Shirt, Audrey Beddingfield, Sheila Liversidge, Pat Taylor, Sheila Unwin, June Hendricks, Ann Speck, Dorothy Walker, Sylvia Thompson, Miss Cross (teacher). Third row: June Harrison, Brian Newbolt, Tony Stanley, Eric Bluff, Ronnie Fleming, Brian Lawrence, Derick Kirk, Jack Glossop, Brian Tindall, Brian Merrifield, Jack Aldred, Jim McNair, Sheila Williamson. Second row: Barbara Whittaker, Jean Stubbs, Maureen Allison, Brenda Smith, -?-, Barbara Tankard, Maureen Stones, Brenda Chapman, Valerie Gilbody, -?-, Beryl Lyons, Beryl Harper, Mavis Ryder. Front row: -?-, Gerald Oldale, Ray Roberts, Frank Clark, Peter Liversidge, Jim Goodwin, Geoff Lyons, Terry Moore.

Above: Frecheville Library was under threat of closure several years ago, but was saved by strong opposition from the public of Frecheville and Hackenthorpe. However, there there was a reduction in the opening hours and the library is now not open at all on Tuesdays and Wednesdays.

Left: The silver gilt Derwent chalice, with a lid date of 1584, is now in the city museum in Weston Park for safe keeping.

The Frecheville Methodist church on Churchdale Road.

Some of the Frecheville shops in 1988, before the post office and letter box moved across Heathfield Road to the new Co-operative stores.

The 1987 carnival procession moves along Smalldale Road.

The band leads the carnival floats along Birley Moor Road in June 1987.

The 1987 carnival queen's float.

The Frecheville Methodist church's sunshine corner queen.

The Frecheville Ladies' Group prefer to stand.

The staff of the Frecheville Library celebrate its fiftieth anniversary.

A friendly wave as the float passes the Spa club.

The theme is Hollywood Greats.

More difficult to find than VR post boxes are Edward VIII pillar boxes (*below*), due to his brief eleven-month reign. Rowdale Crescent is off Somercotes Road, and this pillar box is one of only three in the Sheffield area. There is one on Carter Knowle Road and another outside the Wadsley Bridge post office.

The Frecheville public house on Birley Moor Crescent. Its sign board (*below*) shows the coat of arms of the Frecheville family, who were lords of the manor of Staveley. It was Mr Charles Boot's firm that built the 1,600 houses of Frecheville and who chose the name, but there is no evidence that the Frechevilles of Staveley ever owned land on Birley Moor, so the name given to Frecheville remains something of a mystery.

This triangulation point at the top of Birley Moor is 210 metres above sea level. Looking in a south-westerly direction, one can see the Norton water tower and the tower blocks at Herdings.

A supertram comes across the field on its way to Halfway, May 1995.

This bungalow used to be the weigh office at Birley Vale for the Birley West Colliery.

The Hollinsend sewage works at Birley Vale in 1929. Several buildings in the background are recognisable.

The Rex Cinema opened on Monday 24 July 1939. The first film to be shown there was *Men with Wings*, starring Fred MacMurray, and it was the last suburban picture house in Sheffield to close. The final films to be shown were *Gregory's Girl* and *Chariots of Fire*, on 23 December 1982.

The Intake and Hollinsend social club in 1993 was demolished shortly after this photograph was taken. The Chatsworth Grange nursing care and resource centre has been since built on this site.

The old Royal Oak public house on the corner of Mansfield Road and Hollinsend Road. The new one is built across the corner and is still a John Smith's house.

Around twelve men are aboard the carriage outside the pub, ready for a trip. Almost everyone, including the spectators and the little boy, is wearing a cap. The odd one out is the driver (and probably the owner) of this two-horse drawn carriage.

The Noah's Ark public house is shown on nineteenth-century maps and is possibly older than the Royal Oak.

The Birley Vale tram terminus. An AEC bus waits to come past as the second tram moves to the up line.

five

Birley Spa

The south-facing front of the bath house, seen here after the completion of recent renovation work, which has provided access from the right for disabled visitors with wheelchairs.

The east wall and exit door from the kitchen end of the building.

The north side shows how advantage was taken of the sloping site – the bath itself was situated underneath and there was access from this left hand side. There is also a door on the extreme right, although there was an internal stairway connecting the two floors originally.

Councillor Marjorie Barker, the lord mayor of Sheffield, with Frank Coupe the Town Crier at the top of Birley Spa Lane. The lord mayor is about to unveil the information plaque and declare the bath house and grounds officially open.

*You are invited to join Clive Betts M.P.
at the Official Opening of*

CENTENARY PONDS

in the Shire Brook Valley
at **11.00am., Friday the 18th of June, 1993.**
(location plan overleaf)

R. S. V. P.
*by the 14th June to Sal Pereira, Countryside Management Unit.
Directorate of Planning and Economic Development.
The Town Hall. Sheffield S1 2HH.
Tel: (0742) 735030*

Centenary pond invitation.

The author with a party of visitors, many of them seeing the Victorian bath for the first time.

Mr and Mrs Jowitt, Master and Mistress Cutler, were invited to Birley Spa during Environment Week to perform the opening ceremony, May 1994. The other three, from left to right, are Len Widdowson, Frank Coupe and Alan Bailey (now MBE).

The empty Victorian plunge bath while the renovation work was in progress. This photograph shows the steps and the water outlet at its west end.

Above: The steps at the east end are of a different design. The inlet pipe of the natural spring can be seen just below the top row of larger stones.

Left: An advertisement for the spa.

Below: The other side of the advertisement for the spa.

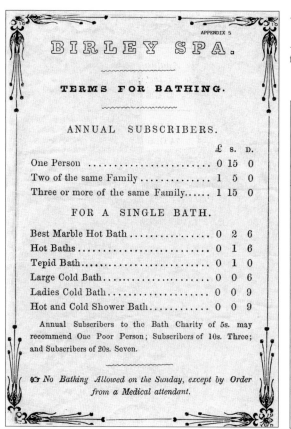

APPENDIX 5

BIRLEY SPA.

TERMS FOR BATHING.

ANNUAL SUBSCRIBERS.

	£	s.	D.
One Person	0	15	0
Two of the same Family	1	5	0
Three or more of the same Family	1	15	0

FOR A SINGLE BATH.

Best Marble Hot Bath	0	2	6
Hot Baths	0	1	6
Tepid Bath	0	1	0
Large Cold Bath	0	0	6
Ladies Cold Bath	0	0	9
Hot and Cold Shower Bath	0	0	9

Annual Subscribers to the Bath Charity of 5s. may recommend One Poor Person; Subscribers of 10s. Three; and Subscribers of 20s. Seven.

☞ *No Bathing Allowed on the Sunday, except by Order from a Medical attendant.*

APPENDIX 4

BIRLEY SPA.

The following is the Analysis of these Springs as made on the Spot,

BY MR. WEST, CHEMIST, LEEDS.

THE LARGE PLUNGING BATH.

Sulphate of Soda .... $7\frac{1}{2}$ Grains per Imperial Gallon.
Chloride of Calcium .. 1 ,,
Carbonate of Lime .. $\frac{1}{2}$,,

Total.......... 9 Grains

This is almost pure Water, *such as is now sought after for the Hydropathic method of cure.*

THE CHALYBEATE SPRING.

Sulphate of Soda .... 40 Grains, equal to 75 Grains of crystallized Glauber's Salts.
Sulphate of Lime.... $22\frac{1}{2}$ Grains.
Carbonate of Lime .. $\frac{1}{4}$,,
Protoxide of Iron .. 4 ,,

Total .... 67 Grains per Imperial Gallon.

The proportion of Iron in this Water is rather large. The Sulphate of Soda present is a valuable addition, tending to prevent constipation and other injurious effects which Chalybeate Medicines sometimes produce when taken alone. The Carbonic Acid present ($11\frac{1}{4}$ cubic inches per gallon) will increase the tonic powers of the Water, as well as cause it to agree better with the stomach.

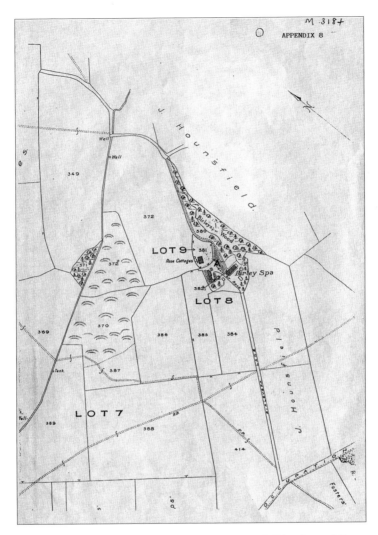

A 1912 plan prepared for the forthcoming auction of Birley Spa and Rose
Cottages. The letter 'A' signifies the position of the water pump. Note
that there was no pond there then.

Above: The retaining wall, built to contain the water as it left the bath house and flowed into the pond.

Opposite above: Mr George Moulson, a local wagonette proprietor, with members of the Siddall family (of Manor Farm, Woodhouse), *c.* 1895. It was Mr Moulson who bought lots eight and nine – 7 1/2 and 4/10 of an acre respectively – for £930. The date of the indenture was 23 April 1913. Terms of the agreement included tenants of the cottages having joint use of the pump and corn rent being payable to the vicar of Beighton – 8s 2d for the bath house and 1s for the two Rose Cottages. It was Mr Moulson who, during the inter-war years, turned the spa and grounds into a local attraction, aptly named the Children's Paradise. (Photograph courtesy of the Siddall family)

Opposite below: The Shirebrook valley, as seen from Birley Spa School playing fields, *c.* 1990. The sewage works in the middle distance have been dismantled, the trees felled and the whole area converted into a nature reserve. Woodhouse is seen in the background.

TREE. DESTROYED. BY. LIGHTENING
AT BIRLEY. SP A. JUNE 9th 1907. PHOTO. BY. J. GOOD.

Above: This group are all dressed in their Sunday best, with the exception of the man on the right, before the pond was there, 9 June 1907. They posed for this occasion after lightning had struck the tree but fortunately missed the buildings.

Opposite above: This photograph was taken in around 1920, when the doorway was in the middle and the building was described at the auction as comprising two cottages.

Opposite below: The north side, showing the old balcony and doorway which have since been replaced by a window. It was demolished many years ago, owing to it being unsafe.

Another front and end view shows the Bath Hotel, as it was known when built by Earl Manvers in 1842. It is in the Dutch style of architecture, which was fashionable at the time. The hotel contained an entrance hall, three bedrooms, a parlour and living kitchen in the middle section, a kitchen and living room at the rear end, and two box rooms, a scullery and the stairway leading down to the baths at the far end.

The wooden dragon, along with other children's attractions, was photographed in 1930.

The same two girls are seated on the bench as their dad appears to be concerned about the boat's safety.

Having decided it is all right, the three set sail on their mini cruise.

This boat was named *Gnat* and behind it is the stone that can be seen on the top of the retaining wall. It was dated 1701, possibly from an earlier building in the grounds.

The pond in May 1993 – the year of its 150th anniversary. The bath house was opened for bathing on 1 May 1843.

Above: From left to right: Alan Bailey, Frank Coupe (in hat and dark coat), Elsie Smith (Labour councillor), Qurbon Hussien (the deputy, and later lord mayor), Sally Peraria (with clasped hands).

Left: Patrick and Dorothy serving on the plant stall.

Children in Victorian dress for the occasion form a circle.

The maypole dancers are ready to start, as Mrs June Fletcher, their tutor, passes by.

Norman Cawkwell, with his band the Sheffield S13 Ensemble.

Police frogmen in the bath retrieving the debris.

The shabby and neglected state of the plunge bath room before the renovation work began. A grant of around £450,000 – donated by English Heritage and the Lottery Fund – enabled work over a two-year period to enhance the whole appearance, both inside and outside of this Grade Two listed building. Earl Manvers would surely have approved. He appointed a committee of four local worthies to run the place: Thomas Staniforth, John Tillotson (schoolmaster), George Cox (of Beighton) and Edward Hobson (of Birley). The latter kept a diary and recorded that the Duke of Portland (from Welbeck) visited with his retinue on 26 May 1843 and took a hot bath. He stayed for a week, taking hot baths daily.

The plunge bath measures around 25ft by 16ft and is around 5ft 6ins deep. The temperature of the water remains fairly constant at 53° Fahrenheit (11.6° Celsius). On 25 March 1843, an advert for a manager and wife was placed in the *Sheffield & Rotherham Independent* and a man called George Eadon was selected. His salary was £20 a year with free coal and rent. Between then and 1912, a further six proprietors came and went. Prices were reduced, but to no avail – by 1895, only the plunge bath remained. Earl Manvers died in 1900 and his son – the fourth earl – inherited the title. In 1912, he decided to sell the property. When he died, on 17 July 1926, the title of Earl Manvers ceased to exist.

Overleaf:
Above: Birley East Pit (Woodhouse Colliery), which ceased to produce coal in 1943.

Below: The excavated site of a Netherwheel Dam building in 1988, known as the Lower Sickle Wheel. The waterwheel was on the left of the two troughs, which were filled with water. The grinding wheel weighed up to two tons, and the grinder sat astride a wooden 'horsing' to grind the sickles and scythes as the stone driven by the waterwheel revolved towards him. This enabled him to apply pressure on the blade through the heel of his hand.

These two industries provided the principal means of employment for the community in the Hackenthorpe area.